REVELATION'S BLUEPRINT & THE STORM COMING

Revelation's Blueprint & The Storm Coming

Lori K Buelow

Contents

Acknowledgment

With deep gratitude, I acknowledge the guiding hand of the Lord, whose Word and Spirit stirred this work into being. To those who walk in discernment and courage, thank you for daring to see beyond the surface and for hungering after truth in turbulent times. I'm especially grateful to the readers, mentors, and fellow watchmen who've encouraged this message and helped refine its voice. Every page is a labor of love, prayer, and persistence. May it serve as a lampstand in the dark days ahead.

1

Prophecy Unfolding

Others have seen prophetic signs throughout history, but nothing like this generation has witnessed, and the final countdown has begun!

Across every continent, systems are collapsing – not from age, but from corruption.

Morality has been rebranded as intolerance. Deception, marketed as diplomacy, and agendas veiled as humanitarian progress.

But beneath all the deception, Revelation's Blueprint is being fulfilled in startling clarity.

As believers, we are not here by accident, but by God's divine plan, and to witness the last chapter of time in God's prophetic countdown.

God has positioned those "watching" with front row seats to Earth's last descent- before the heavens split open and the faithful will be removed in the Rapture like a lightning strike, and Earth will be left to face the consequences it has mocked for generations. God's judgments fall upon Earth as the Tribulation begins.

As the one-world advocates finalize their new system, a throne is being prepared not for peace, but for terror.

The Antichrist will rise, clothed in false Hope and backed by a machine of control.

Daniel's long-prophesied Seventh Week will become a reality as Revelation's Blueprint reveals, and this storm – this orchestrated unraveling- isn't coming: It's already here!

But, before all this happens, we are given indicators of what to watch for as we approach His coming!

2

Watchmen and Those Watching

The term "Watchman on the Wall" is used in the scriptures as an illustration of a spiritual guardian or a bearer.

In ancient times, a watchman was positioned on the "walls" of Jerusalem and would sound the alarm to alert the people in times of trouble.

(Ezekiel 33) explains how God used Ezekiel as a watchman and how he was responsible for warning the people. If he did not, their blood would be upon his hands.

Today, God uses that same ministry by calling out individuals of His choosing to be "watching" for the signs of the times and sounding the alarm as a wake-up call that the prophecy is being fulfilled and the Tribulation is near.

The scriptures tell us in the Old Testament that Issachar's sons were aware of the times, as found in 1 Chronicles 12:32.

Both the Old and New Testaments refer to individuals called to serve as "watchmen."

In our modern times, more than ever, we need to pay attention to those sounding the alarm, telling us that prophecy is being fulfilled.

Watchmen and women have been ringing the alarm bells. Still, today, people are too busy to pay attention or are not interested because they don't believe in the sovereignty of God and His inspired Word regarding what is soon to take place.

That, too, is a prophecy (Matthew 24:10). "At that time, many will fall away from the truth and hate one another." They hate the righteous because they hear the Truth, reminding them of their sinful lifestyle, and making them uncomfortable is unacceptable.

Many today believe the Bible is an outdated book written by man and not God's inspired Word.

Still, God knows those who seek the Truth and want to learn the instructions He has given us in our lifetime for our peace and protection. It is why the term is often used: "To those who have eyes to see and ears to hear." Not to be given to the unregenerate but to His eternal children.

Those with insight into the times today need to stay vigilant and not be overwhelmed by the scoffers and mockers who are emboldened to discredit the Truth foretold in prophecy about the last days.

Prophecy comprises 27-30% of the Old and New Testaments of the Bible. You would think there would be more interest, especially in the churches. Instead, the young pastors in the pulpit today dismiss essential passages in Scripture regarding the Lord's Return, judgment, and sin.

In leading a congregation in this direction, the people are unprepared and living a carnal lifestyle; therefore, they are unlearned in essential aspects of the Bible as Jesus Himself taught.

As the watchmen and women sound the alarm today, "Tribulation is Coming," it falls mainly on deaf ears and will continue as people are distracted by their busy lifestyles or intentionally ignore the message. They will be caught in the snare of Satan he has set for them and will not be able to distinguish "truth" from the "lies," and they will become easy prey for Satan's deception.

In the Seven Letters to the Seven Churches found in the Book of Revelation (Revelation 1-3), the ascended Lord explicitly instructs all individual believers to "watch" for their spiritual development and to be aware of indicators that point to His return.

The Letter to the church at Sardis (Rev 3:2-3) and throughout the ages serves as a "wake-up" call to believers to be on guard, so they don't lose their zeal and enthusiasm for Jesus and become complacent, ignoring the spiritual battle ahead. (Ephesians 6:12).

The call to believers to "watchfulness' is a warning from God the Father to each generation.

Keeping Watch

During Jesus's time on Earth, He gave His disciples many instructions to carry out His teachings; one of them was to "Keep Watch."

What does 'Keep Watch' mean, and what do we watch for?

Keeping watch means paying attention to social, spiritual, environmental, and political events as the current trends align with the prophecies recorded in the scriptures.

To "Watch" alerts us to the nearness of the hour of the soon-coming return of the Lord, and when the divine judgments of God fall upon the Earth, known as the Tribulation period.

The prophetic books of the Bible are like a big roadmap to Heaven, with many pieces scattered throughout. As one grows in their faith and has the desire to understand prophecy, they diligently seek those "truths" that Jesus and the prophets spoke concerning the end times. Then, the scattered pieces begin to fall into place as one seeks to know those "truths" spoken about.

It is one reason why Jesus often spoke in parables to His disciples while on Earth.

When they asked Him, "Lord, why do you speak in parables? He replied, "Because it is for you to understand, and not the rebellious (unbelievers).

It is why those who choose not to follow the Lord on this Earth can never understand or know the closeness of the hour to His return and all the things He foretold would occur; it is also why they scoff and mock you when you try to alert them to the signs of the times as (1 Corinthians 18) says," The message of the cross is foolishness to those who are perishing. Still, to you who are saved, it is the power of God."

Jesus also tells us, "Don't cast your pearls before swine." (Matthew 7:6) He knows those who will listen to you and those who will not.

It is what happened on Noah's Day; they rejected the warning, just as they are rejecting your warning today. You can only warn those who want to know the truth; otherwise, it falls on deaf ears. And when that happens, the Lord said to shake the dust off your sandals and continue your journey, telling those who will listen.

As we "watch" all the "signs" unfolding, they are rapidly converging just as a woman's birth pangs in process, as the prophecy describes.

We must stand against the tests and trials that come our way (Matt 6:41)

To be alert to the devil's attacks and led away into what is not pleasing to God (1 Tim 5:15).

To be aware of false teachers in sheep's clothing.

To live a proper lifestyle on Earth. (Luke 21)

To be ready to meet the Lord on His return (Matthew 24).

3

Peace & Safety

Since President Trump returned to the Oval Office, he has intervened in the Russia-Ukraine perpetual war, the protracted conflict of Gaza between Israel and Hamas, as well as Israeli attacks against Iran, and more.

His global initiatives are fashioned under the doctrine of Peace and Security, which he illustrates as "Peace through Strength," always prioritizing America's national interests.

After surviving an assassin's bullet in Butler, Pa, President Trump is convinced that his presidency is a divine call from God.

Consider the scripture, Peace & Safety in (1 Thessalonians 5:2-3), "For you know quite well that the day of the Lord's return will come unexpectedly, like a thief in the night. When they are saying Peace and Safety, disaster will fall on them as suddenly as a pregnant woman's labor pains begin, and there will be no escape.

Former presidents have tried to bring Peace and Safety to the Middle East, but have failed.

Suppose God divinely appoints President Trump to lead initiatives for Peace and Safety in the Middle East. In that case, he will then be chosen to set the stage for the coming world leader (the Antichrist) to "confirm the covenant."

(1Thessalonians 5:3-5)," When they say Peace and Safety, then sudden destruction is at hand."

That sudden destruction could be nuclear.

Taking a closer look at the scripture, it tells us: "But you aren't in the dark about these things, dear brothers and sisters, and you won't be surprised when the day of the Lord comes like a thief. For you are all children of the light and children of the day; we don't belong to darkness or night.'

(1 Thessalonians 5:9) sheds light, telling us: "For God chose to save us through our Lord Jesus Christ, not to pour out His anger on us."

We as believers have nothing to fear, as a promise is given to us in John 14 that Jesus said just before He was resurrected that "He was going to prepare a place for us in Heaven, and if He prepares that place for us, He will return for us." That is Rapture.

So, as the Tribulation is taking place on Earth, we as believers will be in Heaven as God's wrath is poured out on the rebellious living on Earth.

Considering the prophecy, we now understand that all true born-again believers living on Earth will not be here when the "Sudden Destruction" occurs. Many believe that, in the moment the possible nuclear strike takes place, that is when perhaps all believers vanish, in the twinkle of an eye, as quickly as we are told.

Keeping that thought in mind, once the devastation takes place and millions vanish, the Antichrist then brings a false sense of security to the world, because people will then be looking for answers. He then "confirms the covenant," but only for a short time.

So, what "covenant" does he confirm? Many believe that if President Trump succeeds in arranging Peace and Security between Israel and the surrounding countries, and the Rapture takes place shortly after that, the devastation follows as the above scriptures tell us.

Since President Trump survived the assassination attempt in Butler, Pa, he has publicly announced that he accepted Jesus Christ as his Savior and is a born-again Christian.

Does it relate to the discussion? Yes, it has great significance. If President Trump is divinely appointed to start the Peace and Safety process in the Middle East, and he is a born-again Christian, he will vanish along with all other true Christians on Earth once the Rapture takes place.

The Antichrist, whoever he may be, will then come on the world stage and "Confirm that Covenant" with many, as the scripture says.

Ponder for a moment, the prophecy tells us he "confirms the covenant," and that means a treaty is already set in motion. You cannot "confirm" something that is not there; the policy must already originate.

President Trump's efforts to bring Peace to the Middle East can be viewed as a possible forerunner of setting the stage for "confirming the covenant" with the Beast of Revelation 13.

As it is written in Daniel 9:27, the Antichrist confirms a covenant for one week. (meaning, seven years) And it is the official start of the Tribulation era.

President Trump's Abraham Accords were a tremendous result that established relations between Israel and several Arab countries. However, it did not solve the escalating discourse between Israel and the Palestinians or Iran and its proxies.

President Trump's administration demonstrated how a President can succeed with ambitious peace proposals and significant backing from patriotic and international authorities. He thanks God for the work he is called to do.

Another leader (Antichrist) will rise to power, but he will get his power and authority from Satan, the one he follows, as scripture is clear on it in Revelation 12:9.

Consider the difference between President Trump and other past leaders in their peace initiatives; each one has attempted to bring Peace to the Middle East.

The Beast of Revelation 13 will obtain Peace. Still, in the Middle of the Tribulation, he will break the covenant, and the people of the world will be plunged into a treacherous and terrorizing time as wickedness and worldwide suffering will occur.

The history pages show us how willing followers will embrace and support an inspiring individual who claims to be able to restore order in uncertain times.

If tensions in the Middle East cause people to yearn for Peace, and one person finally appears to be effective, how quickly will others accept that person?

Israel

President Trump has warned that attacks on US allies will have dire ramifications, and the White House has guaranteed to the UN that America will fully support Israel.

Because of America's military strikes on Iran's nuclear provisions, which Israel was not capable of doing because it did not have the hardware, it has somewhat secured itself. It has been implied that Netanyahu should end the War in Gaza.

President Trump and Prime Minister Benjamin Netanyahu met at the White House, and reports have circulated that there are high hopes for Peace in the Middle East after that meeting.

Nobel Peace Prize

President Trump was nominated for the Nobel Peace Prize by Israel's Prime Minister, Benjamin Netanyahu. He asserts that the President establishes Peace in multiple countries, one after another.

He has brought Peace to Rwanda, South Africa, and Congo.

President Trump views himself as a peacemaker and has proven such in the Israel-Iran conflicts, Russia, Ukraine, and other countries.

The Sanhedrin

The Sanhedrin is composed of a rabbinical council of 71 members that aims to revive the ancient Jewish highest court in modern times. It oversees the preparation of the newly built third Temple, including the training of priests and the construction of the altar.

Its goal currently is to utilize doctrinal and national language to influence religious and political thought in Israel, despite not yet having an official position in the government.

The Sanhedrin sent President Trump a letter, thanking him for his intervention in Iran by destroying its nuclear facilities, and told him that he was divinely appointed by God to be a peacemaker for Israel.

The Sanhedrin and the Temple Educational Center minted a silver coin with an image of President Trump engraved alongside a picture of King Cyrus, who in ancient times ended the Babylonian captivity and allowed the Jewish people to return to their homeland.

They are also grateful to President Trump for making Jerusalem the capital of Israel.

A depiction of the Temple is inscribed on the coin's reverse side.

Russia, Ukraine & Peace

The President has talked with Putin on several occasions, yet Putin continues the War, and President Trump has vowed to use sanctions and tariffs against Russia if the War is not resolved.

The United States is acting as a mediator between Russia and Ukraine. Like Israel, President Trump will not cut off America's aid to Ukraine but is continually negotiating in hopes that a path to Peace will emerge.

Putin and President Trump met in Alaska to discuss a peace proposal. Following that meeting, the president met with the leader of Ukraine and the NATO members in hopes that all would agree to peace.

President Trump has been instrumental in bringing Peace to many countries, and we are grateful for that.

However, the true peace that nations are searching for cannot be found in human intervention; it can only be found through Jesus Christ when He returns and sets up His millennial Kingdom.

(Isaiah 9:6) Jesus is called the Prince of Peace, and He alone is whom we put our trust and Hope in.

4

2027 Earth Changing Events

The internet has been abuzz with talk about a defining moment in human history, possibly occurring in the year 2027.

Various voices, including those from prominent investigative reporters, prophecy websites, and whistleblowers, as well as multiple platforms, are discussing 2027 as a moment of reckoning for humanity.

Still, others' question is whether such speculations are true and if there is any merit to all the reports coming forth.

One report stated that 2027 is the year when high-ranking government officials are persuaded that a cataclysmic event will occur. Due to tight security pledges, such individuals remain anonymous as they attempt to alert the public that time is of the essence.

Several ultimate possibilities were presented: a destructive asteroid will plunge to Earth, a geomagnetic reversal, and a devastating step forward in AI that could pose a threat to civilization.

Yet, these were not the only alerts, as other voices have sounded the alarm on electromagnetic interference that could set humanity back to the 1800s, and possibly transform continents.

Claims were made of disturbances coming so great as 'Noah's day during the flood, and massive worldwide weather patterns so severe with winds persisting for weeks at a time, and hailstones so great that they will destroy crops, and full-scale catastrophic national disasters.

These are not just random thoughts; authorities within the government are also making plans for the year 2027 and beyond. NASA has conducted several simulations of possible asteroid collisions for that timeframe.

The asteroid, Apophis, has received much attention on the internet as it will be observable once again in the year 2027, which is when scientists will then be able to track its trajectory for the year 2029 when it will be closest to Earth and remain on the path it's on, or a direct collision course toward Earth if it has shifted.

Consider another alarming claim by Catherine Austin Fitts, a former Bush administration director, during a Tucker Carlson interview, who mentioned that trillions of dollars have been spent building underground hidden bunkers in the case of an apocalyptic event occurring.

She stated that 170 cities exist underground, and some are even located beneath the ocean.

While the high-profile elite silently prepare, could the rest of humanity be racing toward a cataclysmic event?

Steadfast Prophecy

The Book of Revelation, as well as Matthew 24, provides details on weather conditions and End-time events, such as pestilence, fire, famine, earthquakes, major hailstorms weighing 100 pounds, and massive asteroids falling to Earth.

(Revelation 8:1-13) Describe some of those cosmic events to occur; something like a massive mountain on fire falling from the sky into the sea; that description is like an asteroid.

Another cosmic disturbance told in the Book of Revelation is when the third angel blows the trumpet, a great star falls from space upon the Earth with a blazing tail of fire. The name of the star is Wormwood, and a third of the waters turned bitter, and many people died from the waters."

These are not just figures of speech, but genuine, specific judgments, tectonic, environmental, and atmospheric.

Objects such as an asteroid or a star that has fallen from space are not only a chance, but according to prophecy, a fact.

Scientists can track space objects from a human perspective, but prophecies related to such matters are divine and guarantee their occurrence.

Consider the difference between current-day discussions filled with speculation and conjecture, and secrets that high officials in government will not reveal to the public. Prophecy, however, is solid proof, as many prophecies foretold by the prophets of old and Jesus Himself have already been fulfilled and are trustworthy.

(Luke 21:11) Jesus warned us to be "watchful."

How much more explicit can the warning be?

Great earthquakes, pestilence, famines, and fearful signs from heaven.

These are convincing signs to watch for.

The "signs" are given to us so we can prepare and remain steadfast in the loving arms of protection that God promises to His people, while the rebellious of humanity panic and stockpile, in hopes of preventing such horrifying events from coming.

As the 2027 theories are filled with speculation on the internet, we should not be scared, but rather encouraged, because we know the one who holds the future.

(Matthew 24) alerts us to lawlessness, and many deceivers would abound in the last days. Christians are not supposed to be deceived by sensationalism and theories that skeptics devise, but rather remain steadfast in trusting what the prophetic Word of God tells us will surely come to pass, regardless of what mockers and scoffers say.

The Truth taught to us is that one day, soon, the heavens will open, and Jesus will return, and that the sky will shake. On that day, every knee will bow to Him, including those who reject Him now; they, too, will bow their knees to Him.

So, is 2027 the year that an earth-changing event occurs? It is a possibility, but no one knows precisely.

There is one thing we do know and can count on to happen, and that is God's prophetic Word will positively be fulfilled; and that what is written in the Book of Revelation about a mountain ablaze, (possibly an asteroid) will have a direct hit upon Earth, and Wormwood, a name of a star falls from space to Earth causing the waters to become poison.

Consider these not mere speculations, but positive assurances.

So, while the internet is abuzz about the year 2027, we place our Hope and trust in the One who holds the Earth in the palm of His hand, Jesus our Savior, who is coming soon to escort all those who are "waiting and watching" for His return into the portals of Heaven.

We have only a small window of opportunity left to alert others and share the good news of the Gospel with those who will listen.

5

Wars and Rumors of Wars

Wars, Rumors of Wars & Chaos

Matthew 24 Tells of wars and rumors of wars; some will say these things have happened since the beginning of time; indeed, that is true. However, the prophecy suggests that there will be an increase in the consistency and strength of those happenings.

The astonishing parallels between what is happening daily in our world and what the prophetic Books of the Bible say are profoundly woven.

The Ukraine-Russia war is a good example of what the scripture in Matthew 24 refers to: what Jesus suggests will occur in the closing days of history.

World War I and World War II, the Civil War, the Revolutionary War, Afghanistan, Vietnam, and the Gulf War are added to the lists of those observing the "signs of the times" of Wars and nations rising against one another.

Under the previous administration, the world's three most strategic regions were experiencing escalating tensions and major wars that necessitated the involvement of the United States.

The potential for worldwide conflict, including America on one, two, or all three fronts, heightened concerns about the possibility of a third world war.

The looming threat of a catastrophic nuclear war was reported in 2024, as Putin has threatened multiple times to launch atomic missile attacks on NATO and the United States; how much longer till he does it?

As Matthew 24 tells us, nations rising against nations, along with famines, pestilence, and earthquakes in many places, are all indicators of last-day events foretold to increase in intensity.

(Ethnos) It is the Greek Word for a nation and implies conflict among those of various cultural groups.

In areas where substantial Muslim communities are established, the fury of Hamas is often heard among remorseless sympathizers.

Recent reports here in the United States have echoed the caution of terrorists entering the country and sleeper cells among the public; many young military-age men, physically fit, of Middle Eastern descent, as well as those who are indoctrinated into radical extremist ideologies, want to fan the flame of the intifada to suit their cause.

The previous open border policy has allowed our enemies to enter the country, and now, with the recent bombing of Iran's nuclear sites by the United States, the talk of those sleeper cells in our country is a significant concern, as major cities are put on alert.

Racial Issues

The Islamic worldview is to convert the world to their beliefs; until then, fighting will continue, and this is why there is so much conflict in the Middle East and fighting among the different sects and factions in the Muslim world.

The United States faces deep racial divides, exacerbated by poor leadership and extremism. President Trump is actively addressing these conflicts.

These indicators point to the end of days and the blueprint of Revelation, which Jesus foretold would occur just before His return.

Following the Rapture of the Church, the most devastating conflict will break out (Rev 6).

The Lord breaks the Seven Seals, and the second and fourth Seals indicate global warfare unlike anything the world has ever seen. With the increased speculation about nuclear War between two significant superpowers, these are actual, last-day signs; everyone should be concerned.

Israel, Iran, & the USA

The strike on Iran by Israel is more than a country simply targeting another. It is an assault against what is evil, and the Lord oversees everything.

(Psalm 121:4-5) says, "Look, He who keeps Israel will not sleep or slumber. The Lord will watch over you."

The irreligious people (Israel) are at odds with Islam in Israel's fight for survival as a nation; however, the Lord has made many promises to Israel to protect them against their enemies. (Isaiah 31:5, Jeremiah 29:11, Psalm 125:2, Jeremiah 3:17).

The recent anticipation strike on Iran is something that most of the Middle Eastern states welcome, given their concerns about Iran's nuclear capabilities.

Iran may face temporary setbacks, but they are far from eliminated.

Israel will always prevail, even though, at times, things look unclear.

Those of us who understand prophecy know that we are in the end times and that more strenuous times are approaching, according to 2 Timothy 3:1-4.

It is crucial to keep your eyes on Israel because it is God's timepiece for all prophetic events that will usher in the return of the Lord, just after the close of Daniel's 70th week (the Tribulation), which is in the not-too-distant future.

The prophetic books of the Bible imply that Israel will remain in duress and conflict leading up to the day the Lord calls His church into Heaven at the Rapture.

Nations will continue to rise against nations, and the lawlessness will intensify as the world continues to become so depraved and evil that it has reached epic proportions on God's timepiece to make way for the demonic leader of the soon-coming One World government, the Antichrist.

It is then that the Beast makes a deal with Israel for a Seven-Year Peace Treaty. It is the first seal opened in Revelation 6 shortly after the Rapture takes place.

The Peace treaty made by the Beast (Antichrist) will be a false peace, as the World leader breaks this treaty in the

Middle of the Seven-Year Treaty, or 3.5 years, which is exactly 1,260 days into the Tribulation, as he sets up what Jesus calls the "Abomination of Desolation" in the newly built Temple In Jerusalem, (2 Thessalonians 2:3-4), which will be the image of the Antichrist World leader, demanding everyone on Earth to worship the image and taking the mark, (Revelation 13) which without, no one will be able to buy or sell.

As mentioned, by the 70th Week of Daniel, the soon-coming Tribulation continues for Seven Years.

As the end of those Seven Years draws to a close, Satan dispatches his most powerful demonic entities to complete a mission for him found in Revelation 16.

It is the groundwork set for the arrangement of all the kings of the Earth to prepare for the Battle of Armageddon, as troops from all regions gather for the great day of battle. (Zechariah 12:3, Zechariah 14:2-4).

What is Iran's role in this setting?

Iran has joined forces with other countries that are anti-Israel and share the same goal of annihilating Israel. (Ezekiel 38:16), tells of this War.

To understand the severity of the outcome of those countries that come against God's elect, the Jewish nation, in the Battle of Armageddon, one must read Ezekiel 39:2-5.

The battle is so great, and the slaughter of so many bodies upon the fields of Israel in God's fury that He leaves those bodies for every Predatory Bird and the wild animals to devour.

Currently, there is a significant movement in Iran toward the Lord for Salvation as God is summoning His people, and those who accept Jesus as their Messiah will depart with the rest of God's faithful followers at the Rapture, leaving behind an evil nation filled with rage.

Israel will finally accept and recognize their true Messiah, Jesus the Son of God, whom they have rejected over the centuries, when the Lord returns at the end of the Battle of Armageddon with all His people.

He will restore all of Israel, those whose names are written in the Book of Life.

Currently, the United States is a close ally of Israel, mainly due to President Trump.

America had a crushing setback during the previous administration, which was anti-Israel.

Sadly, because of the lawlessness, corruption, and depraved immorality along with the extremists, America has become weak; with the help of churches that seek and support a prosperity gospel in place of the true Gospel of Jesus Christ, President Trump is doing his best to strengthen America. Still, the damage is so significant that it may be too late.

Bureaucrats that are extremist in their "world view" have entirely abandoned the God of Creation, cannot make the distinction between a man and a woman, and have proven to have only half a brain with no genitalia; they march in the streets to protest (they say peacefully) which is a bolden lie and the Marxist media when filming, always pick the places to film where the actual lawlessness and riots are not taking place, then show that to the public and say it is a peaceful protest.

Despite the daily challenges our nation faces, we stand firm in our faith and our freedoms, regardless of the forces that seek to divide us. President Trump is doing his best to maintain Peace, unlike the past administration, which is responsible for the weakening of America.

How can you have Peace when confident leaders rise and promote violence and refuse to govern in protecting citizens?

Have you noticed the slogan used, "No King," at the protest in major cities?

Yet, those that say it have a "Queen," a Drag Queen— a 250-pound male —showing up in a blonde wig and wearing women's clothes at all their events and protests; what is the purpose of such an erotic display?

It is to continue the breakdown of society and remove anything that is left in the land that is true, good, and beautiful. It is to corrupt the minds of the young, as vulgar mentality, ill men who think they are women, display themselves for all to see.

The Los Angeles riots and other cities are showing evidence of a nation that is falling apart, according to the history of other such countries that have fallen from God's blessing and protection.

To ponder the extent of America's decline over the past few years under the previous leaders is thought-provoking.

Under President Trump's leadership, we have only a few years left to tell those who will listen that an approaching storm of judgment is on the way that will usher in the most devastating times spoken of by Jesus Himself, that He said will never occur again. Unless He hadn't shortened those days, no flesh would survive, but for His elect's sake, He shortened the days.

Wars and talk of wars will increase, and the Battle of Armageddon will be the last War fought that Jesus would put an end to at His return; until then, wars will persist.

6

Business as Usual

Individuals observing predictions should recognize the alignment of events on Earth's final days.

Jesus gave, I believe, in Matthew 24, the most crucial of the many events foretold to happen:

It will be just like living in Noah's day. People enjoyed banquets, parties, and weddings until Noe entered the ark. People were not aware until the flood arrived and swept them all away. It will be the same way when the Son of Man returns. Two men will work together in the field: one will be taken, and the other left. Two women will grind flour at the mill; one is taken, and the other is left."

Watch, therefore, for you don't know the hour your Lord will come.

The Lord reveals more about that event so that those with understanding are prepared (Luke 17:26-30).

Likewise, in Lot's Day, He expounds that it will be business as usual in our day. That is, until the very day Lot and his family left the wicked city of Sodom, it rained fire and brimstone down from Heaven on Sodom and Gomorrah.

The day Noah and his family entered the ark, the rain began to fall, and the flood came.

So it will be when the Lord returns to call His eternal family home in the portals of Heaven, it will be "business as usual," and suddenly, the "vanishing" of millions of believers will take place; immediately following, the most terrorizing set of closing day events will commence: Seven Seal Judgments, Seven Trumpet Judgements, and Seven Vial Judgments.

Understanding the indicators of world events related to Bible Prophecy is what the Lord signifies to those searching for "truth" in a corrupt and broken world, as mentioned in the above verses.

Knowing that Jesus walked on the Earth two thousand years ago and foretold all the events happening in our lifetime is miraculous, and for that very reason, He wants everyone to be prepared; sadly, many will perish.

When it was not Business as Usual

Business was not as usual during the four years from 2020 to 2024. America as a nation was on the brink of destruction. The economy was in ruin; the military was depleted; the Southern border was open to everyone, including gangs, drug traffickers, human trafficking, and terrorists of the worst kind, and America's enemies from all over the world were able to enter through.

Our energy was depleted, and our freedoms of speech, expression, and worship were under attack. Censoring online content was out of control, as the public was restricted by what was said unless it fit the narrative of certain groups of individuals.

During 2020, the public watched in horror as businesses and homes were burned to the ground, the elderly were beaten up in the streets, retail stores were plundered, and police were dismantled; as a result, some areas had no law enforcement to keep the Peace and protect innocent citizens.

COVID-19 was released, and lockdowns were enforced; people lost their businesses and jobs, and it became a crime to allow children to play in the park or walk on the beach without being arrested and then forced to take a vaccine that was never tested. As a result, cancers are on the rise in the old and young alike, as well as other diseases that could have been prevented.

Policies and rules were enacted, allowing criminals to be released and victims locked up, as narcissistic leadership steamrolled their plans of fulfilling their Marxist agenda on everyone.

Quality education was removed from public education, and instead of learning, it became an indoctrination center.

Children attended Drag Queen Story Hour, and children as young as kindergarten were presented with sexual topics.

Puberty blockers and mutilation of young children's body parts became part of the curriculum in public education. Parents were not allowed to voice their opinions; their children would be taken away if they did.

The Land of the Free and the Home of the Brave, as most Americans once knew, throughout the years of 2020-2024, were under significant hardship and broken identity, as those who hate the country did everything possible to destroy it.

Sexual orientation, LGBTQ+, and abortion are the platforms that one party ran on the entire time. At the same time, they worked in unison in the dismantling of the country and gaslighting the American people.

Inflation reached its highest level ever, and the housing market experienced a significant crash.

America became a divided nation as extremists in high places promoted race as a weapon in their rampage to divide the country.

A New Sheriff in Town

July 13, 2024, is a day freedom-loving Americans will never forget. It was the day Donald Trump, the Republican nominee for President of the United States, survived an assassination attempt.

God spared his life, and he was elected the 47th President of the United States on November 5, 2024.

In a remarkably short time, things shifted back to "business as usual."

A New Sheriff had arrived, and President Trump began the task of undoing all the radical and insane policies that were previously put in place.

The above Bible verses from Matthew 24 and Luke 17 not only tell us that it will be "business as usual" but also that businesses will be "robust" in activities such as buying and selling, building and planting, and couples getting married. It will be a much better time than usual for the affairs of humanity just before the Lord returns.

It will be a time of great economic prosperity, not a time of collapse as a country, thanks to President Trump, God's chosen leader, to will guide the country out of the brink of destruction.

Not only this country, but businesses worldwide will also be doing quite well.

The poorer countries are less fortunate. However, it has always been that way. Jesus, in His foretelling of the culture just before His return, indicated certain parts of the world that have prospered economically.

The significant financial potential that has emerged is unrecognized by major news media. They continue to harbor enormous animosity toward President Trump.

Still, almost every economic report is currently trending higher in the United States, and the stronger the US economy, the more prosperous other capable countries will become.

The worldwide marketplace is mainly dependent on this country.

Consider, however, that the economic recovery in this country is not based on reasonable assumptions about economics; the massive financial crisis we're in is becoming deeper by the day, and at some point, it will inevitably shatter.

The New Sheriff in town, President Trump, has been divinely appointed by God for a time like this. He is a visionary builder and an exceptional businessman.

The media defies logic and still refuses to present the exceptional upswing in economic growth and stability that America is experiencing.

There is, however, a reason for such so-called journalists to behave unprofessionally.

Consider the fact that reporting on the growing trend this country is now encountering would foil the efforts of the insane, narcissistic individual hierarchy that has worked so hard in the downfall of the Republic of the United States; in other words, such reporting would interfere with the plans of bureaucrats in high places to seize its fortunes and authority to build the worldwide utopia system it so envisions.

President Trump's moves to reaffirm America's position of power are something they are hell-bent on destroying, and not just most media, but those that are against "Making America Great Again" because they are not happy living in a civilized America, but one that is entrenched in Marxist dogma, poverty, and extreme delusional ideologies.

Such individuals are unhappy living in a prosperous nation that offers freedom and rights to all its legal citizens. They should earnestly consider packing their belongings and moving to another country that shares their delusional beliefs. No one will miss them. Go There!

Soon, however, an event will occur throughout the planet: the "vanishing" of all "true believers." Once such an event occurs, the global platform of the Antichrist will be completed, and this is the reason those on the other side hate anything true, good, beautiful, and righteous.

Such individuals are opposed to God and His ways. They demonstrate in their actions that they are their gods and know better than the God of the universe.

When the Antichrist takes center stage, such individuals will welcome that tyrant with open arms, as they prefer darkness to light.

7

Doers of Evil & the Beast System

John 3:20 Tell us: All who do evil hate the light and refuse to go near it, fearing their sins will be exposed.

Unspecified evils have been revealed in America, as President Trump and Elon Musk exposed the fraud and abuse committed by the US Agency for International Development (USAID).

Consider why the extremists and most of the media had a meltdown when the nefarious activities of fraud in government were exposed.

The panic that the extremists displayed was because they had been locked into such extreme measures of fraud for decades.

Evil forces, in conjunction with Deep State swindler cartels, have assisted with kickbacks in funds for virtually every reprehensible movement that bureaucrats are involved in.

Naturally, the mouthpiece of deception media angrily implies that a large amount of the slush fund from USAID was used for a worthwhile cause.

Evidence has come forward that there are radical individuals who use funding to support terrorists.

Below is a short list of some of the causes your tax dollars went to:

Associated Press, Politico, and The New York Times received millions of dollars from USAID. Oddly, these reports were at the helm, fervently reporting falsehoods about the Elections, COVID-19, January 6, and strongly opposing President Trump.

LGBTQ+ received 5 million dollars to advance their agenda, including transgender musical programs, operas, and comic books, and various countries received aid for sex changes from the Biden regime.

Hamas and the Nusra Front terrorist groups had millions of dollars filtered through relief agencies.

Heroin production by the Taliban in Afghanistan and the millions of dollars funneled to Echo Health Alliance aided in the support to weaponize the COVID-19 virus in Wuhan, China.

It is unfathomable even to try to conceive of the atrocities that evil, cold-hearted individuals have committed.

The global elite and their supporters are over their heads in the slush funds, and eventually, all their names will be exposed to the world.

(Ephesians 5:11) Say: Have nothing to do with evil, but expose it.

John 3 tells us, "All who hate the light stay far away from it so their sins are not exposed."

These individuals are not only trying to obstruct the public's disclosure of their malicious behavior, but they are also exerting every effort to argue that the government lacks the authority to disclose such actions.

Marxist Madness Media

Consider for a moment the slogan used by the Marxist media and extremists, that we as a nation were in a "Constitutional Crisis" because of the (DOGE) Department of Government Efficiency.

They spin the Truth and give false information, saying that President Trump does not follow the Constitution because of it.

DOGE was not an agency authorized by Congress; in all their rhetoric, they cannot reference one Instance of Constitutional infringement.

These people are "hollow," and perhaps they should read the Constitution for themselves, starting with Articles I, Sections 2, 3, and 8.

It is the responsibility and right of the President to ensure that their executive branch is held accountable, particularly in cases of waste and corruption.

Not even the so-called experts who were consulted by the Marxist media were able to identify a Constitutional infringement in the DOGE initiatives.

Please allow this thought to resonate: Why was the BBB "Big Beautiful Bill" becoming such a historical policy measure for United States citizens in a generation? It benefits seniors, helps the working class, and small businesses, yet evil doers and propaganda vortex media were exerting every effort to persuade Americans that it is a catastrophe.

It is a spectacular case of gaslighting, where advantages are framed as treachery and truths are concealed under the guise of fear.

Their plan is already prevalent as we approach the 2026 midterms.

They hope that by doing enough gaslighting on the American people, they can continue in their sabotage of President Trump, in their slander and false accusations, and cast doubt on the intentions of the voters who elected him and the Republican majority to office.

You can expect that there will be an ongoing attempt at their gaslighting (which they are experts in), and they will continue in their attempts to punish those who elected President Trump to office by withholding accurate information that benefits all Americans and replacing truth with lies.

The tremendous changes taking place in the country are factual, world-changing events that will take effect immediately, cultivating a better lifestyle for individuals, including those to whom the D.C. bureaucrats have previously disregarded.

With such substantial benefits to the American people, one would think it would be worth reporting. However, as we have witnessed previously, any good deeds done by President Trump have always been met with backlash.

It is in your best interest to ponder for a moment why a "truth distortion chamber" (media) is set up.

Where there is only "resistance" used as a primary goal, gaslighting becomes their main tool.

Consider, if you will, that it is the same strategy in operation as COVID-19.

During the COVID era, dismay and panic were used.

Currently, it is a political ploy designed to distort your perception and undermine your assessment, scamming you into dismissing a move that could protect your future.

The gaslighting will continue on many other topics by the opposers of "truth" and using the "same" talking points, as they do, is not hard to detect if you have "discernment" and walk in truth.

Consider, after almost nine years of media coverage on the Russia Gate scandal, and linking President Trump to collusion with Russian operatives.

In 2025, the discovery of a secret room, "burn bags," and a disposal system was made—the classified documents revealed a politically motivated agenda against President Trump.

Yet, the media "spins" the truth, and the "same" talking points circulate throughout media networks, as the "gaslighting" continues in hopes of causing the public's perception to be dumbed down into the reality of believing the false narrative they propagate.

The deception is what the Lord Jesus warned would come in the last days. He calls it "perilous times," and was referring to this generation.

As mentioned, we are engaged in a spiritual war; it surrounds us, and each one of us is a part of that battle.

It is good versus evil.

Your "worldview" determines which side you are on and asking yourself what freedom truly means will help clarify the good from evil, truth from lies.

Now is the time to sharpen your discernment more than ever, because deception will get increasingly darker through the coming weeks and months just before the Lord returns.

"The prudent person sees danger coming and hides himself, but the ignorant ignore and pass on. Proverbs 22:3

Jesus warned about the prevalence of deception.

(Matthew 24:4) "Take heed that no man deceives you."

Antichrist Beast System

Doers of evil can also be classified as individuals who are working to establish a world system that will eventually usher in the evilest tyrant that will control all of humanity, the Antichrist.

Even though the Antichrist has not yet been revealed, an Antichrist system is being implemented to assist him when he comes on the world stage.

The Globalist intentions to establish a worldwide government have been increasingly transparent during the last decade. After years of dismissal as extremist ideology, the WEF and the United Nations have made their ambitions of global dominance obvious. It is all out in the open now, as they labeled those who previously tried to warn others as crazy conspiracy theorists.

At this time, the Restrainer, the Holy Spirit, is keeping the identity of the Antichrist hidden until the church is called into the portals of Heaven. However, at this time, a group of global elite power brokers is preparing the world's systems for the arrival of the Beast of Revelation (Revelation 13) by ensuring that all preliminary work to facilitate his rise to power will be in place when he is introduced on the world stage to the populations of the Earth.

Klaus Schwab, the director of the WEF, presented at the 2025 World Summit in Dubai his version of the support of governments in what he called the "Intelligent Age."

His plan revealed global participation, the use of AI worldwide, and government overseeing technological advancements.

He highly stressed the regulatory framework globally for crucial digital transformation and the ultimate urgency of all the world's populations to be vaccinated every six months to control health emergencies.

Those who understand the prophetic texts written in Revelation 13 of the Holy Bible can distinguish Klaus Schwab's suggestions from the warnings that foretell an Antichrist Beast System—a New World Order of global governance that will have unprecedented control over the entire Earth.

Klaus Schwab appears to be a key figure in arranging the Great Reset, which has all the characteristics of Revelation 13, the Beast System.

Beast Control

Klaus Schwab presented the importance of all countries regulating AI and advancements in technology. A globally unified framework was a solution he proposed, parallel to (Romans 13:7), which speaks of the "authority" the Antichrist will have over every tribe, people, language, and nation.

A biblical prophecy about a world dictator who will manage everyone's funds globally is echoed in Klaus Schwab's promotion of humanity, which is growing more interconnected through digital means. Revelation 13 describes such a system in horrific terms.

The vision Schwab presented to world leaders on AI and Central Bank Digital Currencies (CBDCs) raises concerns that such a network may be used to impose acceptance of a future global dictator's mandates, exerting monetary and cultural control.

World Vaccinations: The First Step Toward Controlling Health Globally.

In his address, Schwab made several contentious claims, including his support for a Universal Vaccination Program that would mandate vaccinations every six months.

It appears that government outreach in public health policies concerns many people, especially those familiar with the prophecy about the end times.

Governments across the globe have restricted those who declined immunization during the COVID-19 pandemic, ensuring that vaccine mandates are a key subject of contention.

There are concerns that forthcoming health policies may exceed the demand for digital health passports or verification of biometric data for engagement in fundamental financial endeavors.

Potentially leading up to the system of Revelation 13, the beast's mark.

Although immunizations are not necessarily harmful, a system that can be set up to monitor and control people according to their health status raises concerns about what could happen if such equipment is used by the wrong individuals.

Jesus warned that there would be strong deception during this era.

For example, you should think about whether these rules are suitable for people's health or if they are part of an evil plan that could be used by a world government to enforce its laws.

Transhumanism and AI

The impact of AI on societal changes was another important theme of Schwab's address.

He said that to define AI and for people to accept it as part of everyday life, public education is crucial.

Nevertheless, it appears to be more than just an economic change, given the more significant trajectory of AI and its interaction with transhumanism. It may be a change in more than just the financial system.

The very definition of "human" is being challenged.

Considering that Klaus Schwab and his close associates are strong proponents of transhumanism, it should concern most people.

Among the goals discussed at the World Economic Forum is the concept of transhumanism.

Not long ago, Klaus Schwab promoted his vision of merging AI with humans, addressing his goal by stating, "The Fourth Industrial Revolution will connect physical, digital, and biological identities."

It aligns with another ominous verse in the prophetic book of Revelation, where the deceiver, the false prophet, gives life to the Beast's figure, endowing it with the ability to speak and demand that all humanity worship the image.

(Revelation 13:15) "He was then permitted to give life to the statue so that it could speak."

In such a prophetic event, AI will play a part in this chilling system.

The world is being conditioned as AI technology advances, and humans have become comfortable with AI making decisions, where control and digital governance could dictate all aspects of society, including belief patterns.

The doers of evil are anxious to establish the Beast System.

Interestingly, Klaus Schwab announced in the Spring of 2025 that he was leaving his position, and his predecessor will have the same views as he, no doubt.

Biometric Initiative

At the 2025 World Economic Forum, Larry Ellison announced a drastic change in cybersecurity methods.

Oracle plans that within the next year, passwords will no longer be used, and biometric identification will be used instead.

Ellison promoted biometrics, criticizing traditional passwords as outdated and insecure, and biometrics as a safer alternative.

The tech industry is moving toward enhanced security efforts, pointing toward security measures based on particular anatomical traits like fingerprints and face recognition.

Biometric identification can enhance security, but it also brings up issues of privacy and abuse.

If fallen into the wrong hands of people, biometric information can be misused.

Revelation 13 tells how the Antichrist will take control over the Earth. Have you ever wondered how it is possible?

Biometrics is part of such a framework.

Biometric Control

Transitioning to Biometric authentication provides a broader effort aimed at digital identity.

Biometrics replaces paper credentials with an individual's unique set of physical traits, making it possible to gain access to essential services like healthcare, banking, and government resources.

As digital IDs become increasingly essential for travel, banking, and public services, they are already being implemented in many nations worldwide.

Despite the claim that this enhances security, the consequences are far-reaching.

Individuals who fail to comply with specific regulations may be unable to access essential services once biometric access is integrated with financial and social systems.

It reflects the warning of Revelation 13, stating that one must take the mark of the beast to buy or sell.

Those who disagree with the new system may be left out, just like those who don't take the beast's mark during the Tribulation in the End Times.

Digital Spy State

AI was a primary focus of the 2025 World Government Summit, and how it will be implemented in Security, Economics, and governance.

The main topic of several speakers was how AI can enhance public safety, improve government efficiency, and refine governmental enforcement.

Nevertheless, artificial intelligence allows a digital monitoring system unprecedented in history.

AI-powered solutions are being used more by businesses and governments to observe actions, keep an eye on relationships, and forecast behavior.

The combination of AI and a spyware system could be essential in the Antichrist's ultimate domination of the planet.

Caution in (Revelation 13:15) implies that the Beast image will be able to communicate and demand worship, which may refer to an AI-powered policing system.

With significant advances in algorithms for learning, robotics, and deep-state technologies, modern AI is quickly reaching such power.

It points to a time when digital entities may have an actual impact on humanity.

It can be argued that we have reached that point in certain areas.

In the "Intelligent Age" that Klaus Schwab anticipates, digital authorization, biometrics, and a centrally controlled government all work together to increase domination of the world's population.

Christians must understand the fundamental trajectory.

Currently, such technologies and policies are being promoted by laying the groundwork for an extensive control system that reflects the Beast system foretold in Revelation 13.

Christians everywhere must remain observant as these events unfold, staying alert and discerning the circumstances, uncovering the truths spoken in prophecy.

Promoting global control and restraining freedoms should be a wake-up call to believers.

The warnings implemented in the Prophetic Books of the Bible are simple to understand.

Soon, a time is coming when everyone will be expected to pledge their loyalty to a global leader, and anyone who dares to oppose will face severe consequences.

8

Displayed Mockery & Judicial Coup

Bureaucrats cannot admit that a significant majority of Voters in the United States have overwhelmingly rejected a particular party's leadership.

They refuse to consider the reason most Americans have turned on them and are entirely disregarded by the extreme elements of the Party, which is the foundation that governs it.

Judging by their absurdities, it is fair to assume that the radical base cannot solve their problems, as the reasons behind the Voters in this county's decision to reject them during the 2024 Election are worth examining.

Their insane behavior includes shrieking in opposition to and criticisms of everything concerning President Donald Trump.

They display, in their rage, overwhelmingly Narcissistic traits as their behavior incorporates the incineration and vandalism of swastikas, Tesla electric autos, which they recently advocated for, in contrast to the removal of gasoline-powered autos.

They protest the removal of criminal rapists, cold-blooded killers, and child sex traffickers who have entered the country illegally.

The closing of the borders by the President, they seethe at it as they continue to display their madness in the news.

Rather than safeguarding the American citizens (an oath they took), their allegiance is to defend and protect child sex traffickers, murderers, and rapists, which was previously allowed.

Their belief system is characterized by a denial of Reality on every level, including spiritually, naturally, and morally.

They support any anti-God movement that dehumanizes, mocks, and devalues people and normalcy.

Their climate psychosis is like a sacred altar at which they serve Mother Earth.

They advocate for the exploitation of the most vulnerable, which is the children, in every conceivable manner, including the use of body alterations of a child's gender and hormone blockers.

The inherent agenda is to turn the American culture that most of its citizens are familiar with into a representation of a city in ancient civilization, Sodom.

America has always been known for welcoming all those who embrace freedom and national sovereignty, enter this country legally, and wish to assimilate into the American way of life. It has been a beacon light for those who choose to do so. However, it now stands in the way of uniting all countries together under a One World Governance system, of which all who oppose the American way of life have chosen Marxism in place of traditional America.

We are in a cold civil war against anti-God individuals, those who want to transform America into a Socialist/Marxist state.

Nevertheless, God the Father, who sits on His throne in Heaven, has a different plan for dealing with the reprobate-minded people of Romans 1:28, at least for now.

Those who are spiritually attuned to what the ancient text of Bible Prophecy tells us are watching in real-time (Psalm 2:1-5) as it unfolds.

If you are not familiar with the above scripture, now would be a good time to open your Bible and read what it says.

Part of the verse tells us He will put the anti-God supporters on display in mockery for all to see. Those who are discerning are seeing God performing the very thing He said would come to pass as we witness Heaven's actions, while the anti-God people haven't a clue, continuing in their rejection of the Highest and the horrors of their fate to come.

God is just moments away from intervening in this desperately wicked Sodom-like planet, just as He did in ancient times.

Those who oppose all that is sacred are being held in confusion, just as (Psalm 2:1-5) reveals to those with understanding.

The handiwork of God is unfolding throughout the Earth, bringing all things prophesied about the times we live into fulfillment as we witness the fanatical obedience disassembling the essence of their political identity. The source of that is from God's hand, I believe.

Everything we are witnessing is notable evidence of how rapidly things will unfold from this point forward.

Judicial coup d'etat'

Consider the madness of the wave of court orders that have tried to block President Trump's plans to restore order in this country. It is another segment of the cultural decline of the last days, and always the same group of like-minded people demonstrating their actions against Truth, Freedom, love of God, and country.

A Judicial coup d'état was orchestrated in the United States by unelected officials who assumed the position of judges but were political. They needed a conduit to prevent President Trump from rescuing the country from the powers that be. In their insanity, a "Judicial coup" is what they believe will stop the President from allowing criminals to be deported.

Some (not all) in the judicial system have robbed the American people for the past 60 years, and it all started when they took prayer out of school.

They look through their books and pick a "topic" they can use, then put a brand on it to call their own and run with it. They used unelected officials who assumed the position of judges and used that power to uphold their agenda at the time.

Abortion was the "bundle" they used in the courts for the past 50 years. The new "bundle" used now is the Rainbow Jihad.

Evil does not stop itself. It must be stopped!

As mentioned, such people oppose anything true, good, and beautiful.

They want an "Interplanetary Constitution," not the American Constitution.

(2 Timothy 3:13) "However, pretenders and evildoers will thrive. Not only will they trick other people, but they will be deceived themselves.

9

Deception, End Time Sign

On the Mount of Olives, when Jesus sat, His followers approached Him in private and inquired, "What sign will signal your return and the end of the world?" His reply was,' You will be arrested, and you will be subjected to persecution and death. You will be despised worldwide because of your association with me. Numerous individuals will abandon Me and harbor animosity toward one another. Additionally, countless false prophets will emerge and deceive others. Sin will be rampant everywhere. But those who endure to the end will be saved.

The Gospel's Good News will be preached worldwide so that all nations will hear it, and the end will come.

Jesus tells of many more signs to watch for, but because "Deception" was the first sign He warned about and is so prevalent in our society today, I want to address it.

As God's children, we are blessed by the Holy Spirit to discern trouble and deception when it comes our way, and we see it daily, if not hourly, on major news networks, social media, government, academia, families, and even churches.

Unbelievers, even since something is not right in our culture and families, are significantly divided against those who hold to a biblical worldview and are awake to the deception. Those who have a "worldview" and are woke choose to believe the falsehood presented to them by the other side. A genuine separation exists, as Jesus said it would occur.

It is a sad fact that deception is rampant in churches today, as many have bought the lie of "inclusion," which opposes the Gospel as the Bible presents it, and has replaced it with a twisted version, as many church members embrace a world system and no longer hold to a biblical worldview.

God is love, but He has also given us guidelines to live by, and He said, "No one comes to the Father except through Me" (John 14:6). He tells us He is the only way to Heaven; without Him, no one enters. Yet, it is now considered a "hate" statement to say Jesus is the only way for those who have chosen to make up their own set of rules. Heresy has now infiltrated many modern-day churches.

What counts is telling the truth. Doing what is right is essential. Even if the ruling class fails to deliver justice, you can be sure that God will.

We must not tire of standing up for justice.

A Dark Spiritual Battle

What we have experienced in the culture over the last five years under the previous administration is beyond human planning, as the magnitude of evil has never been seen in the history of this country.

The level of deception requires beings and entities beyond us as a species. Humans alone can't do what has been done without the help of a greater evil force at work.

It's like a subplot in a political thriller in the 2020 election, winning six states he never visited, and two weeks later, the mail-in ballots pouring in, as truckloads delivered them and pulling out tubs of ballots from under the desks of so-called workers after taping up the windows, still, caught on camera, for all to witness.

If anyone dared question the validity of the 2020 election, it would be prison time for such a person! They had to have a cover-up and used President Trump as their scapegoat, and COVID-19 was used to shut the country down and control society under a false narrative. Of course, once again, an arrest would be made if anyone dared speak the Truth on that.

Woke and DEI spread like cancer, infiltrating schools, businesses, healthcare, government, homes, and churches.

Biden's health decline while in office was also denied. On the other side, along with the agents of an agenda media, the Truth was covered up as we watched the frail person in the office stutter and fall routinely in his daily duties. Yet, all the trips to his home in Delaware were ignored and dismissed as misinformation by those who spoke out about it.

Then it is announced that Joe Biden has cancer that has spread to his bones. The type of cancer he has can be detected early, and being President, you would think they would have spotted it long before, so late in the announcement that it was in stage four of cancer when they announced to the public in late May of 2025.

It makes sense now that he has made trips to his home in Delaware on weekends while in the office. Why were his chemo treatments held in secret? Could it be he was going home on weekends for such treatments? Many people are finally waking up and understanding how we, as a country, have been lied to by our overlords. Those lies have been so extreme and plotted that, once again, only dark forces and entities beyond human reasoning have infiltrated those who chose to profit and mislead the American people in such significant levels of distortion.

Many people have come forward with testimony about who was running the country under an incompetent president from 2020 to 2024, as well as the use of the "autopen."

These are only part of the bigger picture of lying and misinformation that the American public has experienced.

Children are being indoctrinated to despise and reject their parents by a deceitful program that masquerades as education in some school systems. Additionally, the system under the previous leadership deceived many parents into believing their children did not belong to them but were the property of the community.

People are deceived and led astray into thinking that the government always has their best interests at heart. Some would even embrace the government as their God has the final say in all matters of their lifetime, including what they eat, where they live, what school is best for their children, medical choices, and where to worship; as the bureaucracy who decides all matters for you, gets all the wealth from others and gets credit for telling (the so-called Truth, and doing the right thing).

Society today has been misled by an agenda that suggests we can resolve all of humanity's issues on our own, apart from God. Instead, greater regulations, greater involvement from the government, stricter control, fewer personal liberties, and universal Peace would solve all our problems.

Contrary to popular belief, some oppressors are collecting wealth at the expense of our liberties and, in numerous instances, attempting to remove many under the pretense of medical treatments.

There is another lie spoken by elites: if the Earth were not so inhabited by humanity, they could rescue the planet. They believe themselves to be guides, the gatekeepers of Planet Earth.

They advise the populace against procreation, although they engage in it themselves. They inform the public about homeownership while showcasing a variety of properties. Even when they warn ordinary people against marriage, the children of the privileged continue to tie the knot. They claim that no one needs their privacy, but somehow, they manage to hide many secrets. They preach anti-car propaganda while flying across the globe in private jets.

They are deceivers, having advanced their falsehoods to such an extent that the Truth is neither desired nor required.

Once again, it is the "deception" Jesus clearly warned us about, and the reason He said to be "watchful" because the deceit would be so great that it would be convincing to all earth dwellers, especially those living in our era, which is the generation that will witness Revelation's Blueprint come to pass before God's wrath is poured out during the Tribulation upon all those who chose to reject the Truth.

Those seeking the Truth, who read the Word of God, pray, and understand Jesus is the Way, the Truth, and the Life, are anchored in Him and have no need to worry about God's Judgments because they are forgiven.

Jesus is the "Truth." He reveals Truth to those who belong to Him through His Holy Spirit, and they cannot be deceived because they discern Truth from lies.

The Truth of the whole matter is that God does not want anyone to perish but to come to His Son and confess they are sinners in need of a Savior, Jesus, who died on the cross for all.

As Satan's grip on the world widens, the believers feel its darkness; falling away, being confused, giving in, and being persecuted are all ways the enemy is attacking believers.

The assaults are personal and echo prophetic warnings.

A period of tremendous deception will increase according to prophecy, and only those who are firmly grounded in Jesus Christ will be able to survive the storm coming. Matthew 24:24

Even though we are aware that more hardships are on the way, we can take comfort in the fact that Jesus already knows our weak state.

Even though the Tribulation is drawing near and darkness is gathering across the land, God's people need not worry, and we shall not fear evil, even in the valley of the shadow of death, because we know the Lord Jesus is with us. Psalm 23:4

Although we are not guaranteed a world free of darkness, we are assured that light will shine through it!

10

The Framework is Set

God has placed President Trump in office to fulfill the end-time prophecy, as all the "signs" are converging rapidly.

President Trump is a visionary who knows how to get the job done. However, the President cannot solve all the problems of evil and sin in our nation; he cannot change the course of a generation that is both evil and corrupt.

Regarding the liberties that the West proclaimed, the United States is the only country on the global stage.

We would have joined the other Western democracies that have surrendered to the Islamic faith or totalitarianism had it not been for President Trump.

Most people are unaware of the severity of America's Judgment under God.

Why do I say that?

The LGBT power in the culture is a relentless judgment against our society.

When the highest court in the land legalized "gay mar-riage," it was an even more substantial penalty.

Our culture may be on the far side of recovery because of a lack of resistance. At the same time, the youth in our na-tion were recently mutilated by gender surgery as a business advantage.

Our deficiency in faith may have permitted God to con-sider the country unsalvageable, thereby allowing for its de-terioration as God withdraws His hand of blessing.

When a culture was overrun by rampant debauchery in the early bible days, God would send His strong and power-ful prophets to warn the people of impending judgment.

Unfortunately, there are not many pastors today who warn of the consequences of sin and call for repentance so that God may remove His hand of judgment upon the na-tion.

The Reality of the Matter,

The extremists are not going anywhere; they are plan-ning the world's future and have plenty of time to do so.

Why are nations so angry? Why do they waste their time with plans? The Kings of the Earth prepare for battle; the rulers plot together against the Lord and His people. "Let us break their chains, they cry, and free ourselves from slavery to God."

But the One who rules in heaven laughs. The Lord scoffs at them. Then, in anger, He rebukes them with fierce fury. For the Lord declares, "I have placed my chosen King on the throne in Jerusalem, on His holy mountain." (Psalm 2)

The enemies of the Lord are instruments of evil. They will continue in their schemes to plot, badger, and oppress the culture until there is no faith left in anyone because of being so overwhelmed with the hardships of just trying to survive daily. They will achieve authority over those who oppose their unconstitutional rule and annihilate them, but only for a short time.

We have witnessed the assaults, unlawful legal matters, court, and everything else they have tried to put on President Trump, including two assassination attempts, and all have failed.

These four years President Trump has been in office do not concern them because they have incredibly influential and affluent individuals who support their agenda.

They will reestablish their authority over their political control and impose their agenda on us with horrific brutality, putting an end to all semblance of liberty for all.

Regardless of how powerfully you present information backing up your evidence, their credibility is diminished, but they will still emerge as conquering heroes, just as we saw with the 2020 elections. For four years, we watched in horror the almost destruction of the United States of America.

A particular political party in this culture represents the culture's condemnation of their rejection of the Christian God in the Bible and His Son, Jesus Christ.

They refuse to accept the written Word of God, and if they claim to do so, they twist it. It is always present.

They have a better way, their way!

Such people can never be defeated, and evil will not stop, but just like cancer, it will metastasize unless it is stopped!

Unfortunately, there are just too many of them and so few of us.

A study throughout the ancient text shows how God dealt with depraved societies, showing His viewpoint: like our enemy, the devil, those who oppose God are the workers used to usher in God's destruction, and it is at that time He will deal with such individuals and vindicate those who follow Him.

United Nations & Redefining Laws

People with a Reprobate mindset are unable to make rational decisions; instead, they tend to be destructive.

If you delve into research on the UN International Law Commission, you will be astonished to learn about such plans.

Plans are already in place as they wait patiently to regain their authority.

A framework has been established that defines "Crimes against Humanity" as actions that undermine the principles of social justice.

To legislate their absurdity and bind their people to it, they need lawless leadership, and they already have support in some places.

It seems they are sure to regain power shortly, allowing them to censor the Truth about their evil actions.

When their henchmen take over the world, they plan to legislate "new protections" for the "marginalized" who are not mistreated; the issue is that most lack faith in God, and it is for this reason that lawlessness and godlessness abound.

We have already witnessed a track record of how corrupt individuals can twist any law to benefit evil and punish the righteous.

Bracing oneself for the supposed redefinition of laws by the UN for the year 2029 is advised, as research is encouraged.

In the not-too-distant future, corrupt world leaders will succeed in their annihilation of every aspect of God's law given to humanity to live by and their venomous attacks on His justice.

As a substitute, they will proclaim the offenses of particular groups of people and penalize with considerable severity those who oppose them.

Christians and the country of Israel are their target.

Israeli leaders and citizens will be accused of being inhumane whenever their country takes action to protect itself from those who hate them, and such a prediction is a proven conclusion because we are currently witnessing it daily.

Christians will eventually realize that we are a scourge upon the Earth that must be eliminated; the Antichrist mob will make sure of that.

In ancient Roman days, they condemned Christians as being enemies of humanity, and the Romans themselves were caught up in all the detestable immoralities possible.

In our culture today, we are seeing the resurfacing of a godless, lawless society as it was back then.

The two selective groups the UN will not impose "Crimes against Humanity" on are Muslims and the LGBTQ community.

The United Nations will step in to uphold the LGBTQ society and make sure they will never hear the Gospel to compel them to repentance. The "Days of Lot" will be ushered in by them to overthrow the God of Creation.

The legislation will guarantee that the agenda of the LGBTQ community, together with its associated entities, is neither restricted nor subject to criticism.

Such laws will not affect Muslims, as they are also classified as protected by legislation.

The United Nations only commits to such laws to further their plans for a One World Utopia, and they are using specific groups of people to establish their godless beliefs upon the entire planet.

Such specific groups of people are convenient tools used for their purposes to establish the World system they will usher in; however, in the end, there will be only two classes of people: the elites and the serfs.

Above all else, they are focused on one goal: the eradication of the Gospel of Jesus Christ and those who commit to it.

Furthermore, eliminating Israel is a top priority for them since the Jewish state stands in the way of their utopia of global governance.

The new redefined laws will penalize those who inform others about what the Gospel says regarding repentance, potentially infringing on civil rights.

They intend to silence the Truth and enforce the "hate crime laws' to target Christians.

As mentioned, they intend to install another member of their side in the Oval Office in 2029, and the Constitution, as we know it, will become obsolete and replaced with a "Universal Constitution" as they see fit to regulate the World in their One-World Alliance.

The only thing we can do at this time is pray against spiritual darkness and share the Gospel of Jesus Christ with others.

America has been overwhelmed by potentially extremely dark gaslighting from those who oppose sovereignty, and with the help of misinformation and spin by media, that it may be we as a country have reached the era I suspect repentance may be extremely unlikely "corporately speaking" as a country; and understanding past generations in early biblical days experiencing the wickedness as we see today, has always been Revival or Bust!

It does not look like we, as a country, and the rest of the world for that matter, are on the straight and narrow path toward revival; that being said, it might be a good idea to prepare our hearts and minds to be targeted by the Anti-God crowd and pray we are "worthy to escape all those things" Jesus warned about!

11

What's on the Horizon

Under this President, we have a small window of opportunity to be a witness for Jesus Christ and alert others about an approaching storm on the horizon if the other side has its way.

Big Tech will no longer censor us under the current administration, as it did during the previous one, but it will not last long. So, please do what you can in the little time we have left to be a light in a dark world.

As we look toward 2029, the forces that once sought to suppress liberty and cloud the human spirit may attempt a resurgence. But history has shown us that darkness cannot extinguish the resolve of the awakened.

Though challenges may arise, threatening our freedoms, laws, and moral compass, it is in the fire of adversity that true courage is forged.

It will be a time of relentless madness once those forces begin to rule with overwhelming remorselessness for Conservatives and Christians.

It will all culminate in extreme moral decay incited by the malevolent global hierarchy and Mystery Babylon spoken of in Revelation 17, leading to the era foretold by Jesus as "the time of Jacob's trouble" during the Tribulation, also known as "Noah's Day."

The Western nations have been weakened by the arrival of millions of illegal immigrants who were allowed to enter the countries by nefarious bureaucrats.

As mentioned, the President is doing his best to repair the damage done, but he can only do so much within the limited time he has left as President.

America's supremacy may have rebounded, but only for a short time, as extremists are working diligently to accelerate the country's weakening.

In other Western nations, such as the UK, Western Europe, and Australia, among others, it may be too late for them to rebound, as radical, extreme ideologues have overtaken the power they once held.

If the other side does regain its power in the next election, this time it will be vengeance that one has never witnessed in a once-free society.

Rapture & Church

It is my opinion that the Pre-Tribulation Rapture of the church is imminent. By 2030, the great falling away from the church will be nearing its conclusion, as we are already witnessing the prosperity gospel and seeker-sensitive movement throughout Christianity, replacing the true Gospel of Jesus Christ.

Many within the church believe that if you are good enough and do good works, as well as proclaim that you think Jesus is who He says He is, and attend church weekly, you will make Heaven; such people are Social Christians, not Committed Christians.

They are deceived because they are carnal in their thinking, nor do they live for Jesus daily; they have never made Jesus Lord of their life, nor do they consider, as Jesus said, the cost to be His disciple.

It will be tough to be a faithful follower of Jesus Christ after the Rapture, but many will do so, and at that time, it will cost them their life under the Anti-Christ regime.

During the Tribulation period, those who become faithful followers of Jesus will start to oppose "Mystery Babylon" (the World Religion), and the technology used by the ruling class will come from Satan.

Humanity will be deceived by the false wonders and miracles the false prophet performs, according to the prophecy in the Book of Revelation.

He will mimic the miracles Jesus performed, causing the blind to see and the lame to walk, and AI will be the technology used.

Those people who have rejected the "truth" they once heard about Jesus will have already been given over to reprobate thinking, and it will be too late for them, and they will believe the lie told to them by the false prophet and antichrist. (Romans 1, Revelation 13,14).

Being a Christian under the new system, believers will be ridiculed and viewed as people who are obstructing humanity's progress toward enlightenment, and their acceptance rating in the world will be lower than that of the worst felon.

Under the new system, those who resist the new Babylonian church and support Israel will be hated by Earth's inhabitants, and that hatred has already begun.

Once the advancement of technology accelerates during that time, the rebellious people who work under the New World system, run by the world leader, will have no intention of assisting ordinary people in the world, as they have only one goal: to deceive humanity.

The Bible tells us their plots and planning will be vastly fortunate. Suppressing any "truth" in their schemes will succeed mightily because of the technology used, which is so advanced; the hindrance to sharing the Truth of the Gospel with others will be critically altered.

The large number of societies that have rejected submitting to Jesus and repented of their sins, including the agents of an agenda media, have chosen to demoralize those who accept the Truth and ostracize them in cruel ways before the public; they gleefully enjoy it.

We see it in entertainment, social media, and certain news outlets currently, and it will get much worse because Satan hates those who are good, as do his followers, because they love the darkness over the light.

In the not-too-distant future, all those who have chosen the "right way" will lose their civil rights and freedom as they will be violated by the "redefining " of the laws put in place under a one-world government, with the worst tyrant in history ruling over humanity, according to Revelation.

In the meantime, Satan will be leading his wicked supporters to construct a "political cause" to legalize the removal of all true believers who are a hindrance to their new system that stands in the way of social justice and opposes their agenda.

The International Court will be the headquarters where believers will be tried. Of course, Satan is the mastermind behind their plans, as Christians will be handed over to and severely persecuted and disposed of through martyrdom according to Revelation 19.

The new law enforcement system worldwide will not charge those who commit real crimes; instead, it will apprehend and punish all those who disagree with its new social justice laws.

Crimes against humanity will be those they call racists, Climate deniers, Homophobes, Zionists, and anyone else who opposes them under their new agenda, which they are working so hard to establish. At the time appointed, everything predicted will become operational and a reality.

We are already witnessing hatred rising against those they label in their name-calling.

The social, economic, political, and moral decline in the United States is already underway, despite President Trump's efforts to reverse it.

The next opposing Presidential candidate picked to run in the 2028 election will be the most contemptible extremist that will emerge, and given their previous track record of disrespecting the process of voting, it should not be a surprise to anyone.

Queer Liberation & Defunding the Police

It is another tool that Satan uses to weaken the country.

What a person chooses to do in the privacy of their home is their business once they reach adulthood.

It does, however, become a significant concern to others when such people are not able to control themselves and choose to engage in sexual acts in public places such as bathhouses, parks where people enjoy walking, children playing in the playgrounds, public restrooms, and rest areas.

Most of the population does not approve of such depraved individuals committing their vulgar sexual behavior in public places, which is why the police are notified, and arrests are made of those people who commit such acts.

They complain and call for the defunding of the police because they are arrested and not allowed to engage in their deviant behavior by openly displaying their perversions in public.

Tolerance

Consider when one group calls for "Tolerance" to all people, yet never lives up to the message they proclaim.

As mentioned, most of society does not agree with individuals who display lewd acts in public places and are not of the same sexual persuasion. Yet, deviants who engage in such behavior expect everyone to approve and respect their choices.

There is more to this matter, however, as hidden beneath the surface is a constructed plan to dominate everyone living under the new system in their delusional ideology.

The goal of the worldwide government when it seizes power during the Tribulation is to regulate laws that allow social decay to spread throughout communities so that everyone is inundated and accepts their perverse behavior, and anyone who opposes them will be punished and arrested.

It is all part of a well-organized goal to weaken the sovereign nations.

During the Tribulation, under the new system, the goal will be for the LGBTQ community to dominate the world. Jesus foretold this when He said it would be like the Days of Noah and the Days of Lot.

During that time the goal of the supporters under the Antichrist system will be to intensify a radical LGBTQ agenda and indoctrinating the very young into their ideology to serve the purpose of the breakdown of the family, (God's structured family) so that it will be so overwhelming to anyone who is left, clinging to their faith, will be destroyed because of the harsh penalties they will face.

The Lord also referred to this era in history as "Perilous Times," and one cannot deny that we have already witnessed, in "real time," much of it unfolding. If the Lord has already warned us of such a time, shouldn't more people be paying attention?

There are only two Worldviews, and everyone who has reached adulthood belongs to one of these: a Worldview or a Biblical Worldview.

A Biblical Worldview is about believing and living in this world according to what the Word of God says humanity is supposed to do. Such people love anything true, good, and beautiful, and believe in Nature's God and the Laws of nature.

A worldview is opposed to God and His view on what He says. They are gods unto themselves and set their own rules and laws, as they love the darkness more than the light.

Your worldview is your destiny. It is who you are and the character you display to the world.

(Romans 1) It is very clear and cannot be denied.

I believe God's Word over man's theory.

In summary, what is occurring and to come:

They will come back with a vengeance, showing no mercy or kindness to anyone who opposes their agenda.

Threats have already been reported by sources that once they regain their power, they will seek revenge on those who opposed them.

There is a strong likelihood that the other side will win the 2028 election, so if you love God, country, and your freedoms, you must do all you can now to prepare and tell others who will listen.

The new system that is to come will be a global empire, as envisioned by supporters of the soon-coming Antichrist, a one-world government spoken of in the Bible set to be operational by 2030, according to sources involved.

People of the Earth will be overwhelmed by the lawlessness and violence they will endure as the "Days of Noah" will be upon us.

The WOKE culture is currently fading, but will return with an unprecedented vengeance, and sexual perversions will be on steroids as in "Lots Day."

The Ten Kings (Ten regions) will be formed, as spoken of in the Books of Daniel and Revelation, and they will give all their power to the Beast of Revelation 13 (the Antichrist).

Pastors will no longer preach the Gospel of repentance and acceptance of Jesus as Savior. A seeker-friendly and prosperity gospel will replace it.

The love of many will grow cold as sin escalates, and most of humanity will be overcome by darkness because they refused the light.

The totalitarian evil government run by the (Romans 1) enforcers will bypass our Constitution, and a Universal Constitution will be the new law for all to live by.

Because of the social unrest and corruption used by Marxists to weaken a once strong city, NYC, it is becoming unrecognizable and soon to be unfit to live in; and as sovereignty is opposed and socialism preferred by such leaders as their inner cities deteriorate; The current President refuses to go along with their delusional plans, there is a strong possibility that the UN will move its headquarters out of NYC, and Babylon Iraq could be the location they choose for their new organization.

If the UN were to relocate its headquarters, all the wicked degradation would be there. The Book of Revelation warns about a revived Empire in the last days, and if it is in Babylon, it will be the city from which the Antichrist rules.

We cannot rule out the possibility that the present UN may crumble and, worse still, a more depraved organization may be established.

The new Vaccine Passports, central bank digital currency (CBDC), and Digital IDs will then become mandatory for the economy and the world.

The new economic system, which is Economic Babylon, will be the dominant power of the world; and to take part in commerce, and survive under that new system, one will be required to take a "mark" on the right hand or forehead; without it, it will be impossible to buy the basic items one needs to survive, as well as to sell them.

Revelation 17 also refers to Mystery Babylon (Religious Babylon). The Global Elite have unified in their creation of a unified global religion that accentuates "Mother Earth: and impairs the Christian Judeo faith.

The new unified religion's goal is to redesign morality, focusing on shared values and environmentalism as substitutes for traditional values.

The call for a unified global movement of religion and spirituality is most evident in UN-supported educational initiatives worldwide.

The late Pope Francis was most outspoken on such a movement and stated just before his passing that different faiths are like different communications, all manifesting the heavenly." All faiths are paths to the Almighty, he said.

The Pope, however, is not a single voice uniting the religions worldwide.

Political and religious leaders are involved in transforming the globe, using shared values and Mother Earth as a baseline for restructuring their global empire.

The upper class in the religious world has for years expressed concern for "Mother Earth" as the primary force for saving the planet.

They advocate for all populations and cultures worldwide, except those who hold a "radical view" that is not aligned with their unity for globalism and environmentalism (climate control).

Those they classify as radical religious views are not accepted, and beliefs that Jesus Christ is the "way" to Heaven are high on their list as considered radical, extremist views.

The same interests and involvement were discussed by Alice Bailey, founder of the Lucifer Publishing Company, an occultist whose numerous manuscripts helped structure the UN and its current spiritual and global transformation of the world.

Channeling the spirits of "Ascended Masters," Alice Bailey claimed, was her calling and had a profound influence on shaping her belief in universal consciousness, which she believed is revealed under all religions, and that all humans are gods. She is a foundational figure in the New Age Movement.

She asserted that the "great heresy of separateness" is a significant obstacle, that being, Christians and Jews.

The Vatican, in its "interfaith" movement, has a global network of rapidly growing religious institutions.

The institutions cover the whole spectrum and are funded by the UN, the wealthy ruling class, and various governments.

Many different religious backgrounds, including, but not limited to, interfaith, spirituality, Islam, philosophy, and paganism.

How do they all find common ground? They are simply trying to incorporate people into what the hierarchy is calling a New World System.

It is the world leaders who are advancing this agenda, even though the media remains silent.

The goal in the unified world religion is to redefine sin and marginalize those who oppose their progressive interfaith movement as extremists.

Canada Arrests Extremist

As the insanity continues to worsen, Canada is overtaken by such progressive policies that a spokesperson for the RCMP, Canada's National Police Force, claims that if an individual switches from liberalism to traditional values, they may be showing signs of extremism.

Ponder for a moment: Under the leadership of Canada's Prime Minister, Mark Carney, you are deemed a national security risk if you hold to the traditions of your parents or grandparents.

It is not speculation, but a new reality: political leaders deeply entrenched in a dark ideological worldview and an increasingly dystopian country.

According to a Staff Sgt. Camille Habel's shocking announcement after the arrest of four people entangled in "ideologically motivated extremism" in Quebec.

She suggested that, instead of focusing on crime and actual credible threats, a simple shift from abandoning progressive policies and adopting traditional family values may be considered a red alert.

Take this to heart: Desiring your children to be reared by their biological parents or believing in the existence of only two genders is now considered a national security risk in 2025 Canada.

Please allow this to resonate: It is not about the general well-being of the individual as they masquerade to the public; it is about totalitarian ideological control by a dark liberal establishment.

The establishment has overwhelmingly advanced to a point in its progressive ideology that its brazen thought process has become Narcissistic on every level, so much so that our so-called overlords believe they have reached God status and are now entitled to diagnose each individual's fundamental moral beliefs.

Today, in modern-day Canada, traditional values like family, faith, duty, and self-sacrifice will get you labeled as a possible threat to humanity and arrested for extremism.

It is not the average Canadian who is indoctrinated in a radical ideological worldview; it is the ruling class that is radicalized into believing anyone who adheres to patriotic conviction, the love of God, and the laws of Nature's God is a suspect and flagged.

It is the government that monitors potential threats to its soon-to-be New World Order, which is already halfway complete and aims to be fully established by 2030.

In the meantime, in 2025 Canada, Christians have been arrested, arsonists have burned down churches, and lawless mobs roam the streets, yet the political class and Canada's Police do not appear concerned; but dare oppose their gender ideology or try to be a parent and raise your children, and the authorities may be knocking at your door.

The Progressives call it progress, and anyone who can still think for themselves and make rational decisions understands it is called a PURGE that is taking place.

The same playbook is being used worldwide, and the propaganda is masked, as mentioned, under the guise of "public safety."

The "redefining" of laws will continue as they advance their "unified world religion," and accusations against those who still hold to traditional beliefs will intensify.

Canada is just a stepping stone in the attempted radicalization of their dark, dystopian ideology.

What is happening in Canada is a repeat of a global trend, as the same playbook is being used across other Western nations, from Germany to the United States, from educational institutions to courtrooms.

The goal is to publicly shame those who believe in traditional values, right and wrong, and target the family as they prioritize in destabilizing truth.

Now is the time to take a stand for your children, grand-children, and great-grandchildren, if you have not done so, because time is running out.

Don't allow individuals who are impaired in their thought process to scare you into stumbling and not believ-ing in truth and reality.

There is already a divide here in America and around the world.

A spiritual divide is occurring, and we are engaged in a spiritual battle, and everyone is involved.

It is no longer a matter of left versus right. It is good ver-sus evil.

12

The Final Generation

This generation stands out from all others, as it appears to be embracing evil at an alarming rate.

The teachings of Jesus reveal the truth of a future generation, as foretold by the apostle Paul.

It is a prophecy given by the Lord regarding the generation that will be among those who are still alive when He intervenes in the wicked activities of humanity.

The situation will be the same as it was when Lot was living in Sodom, as described by the Lord Jesus.

"And the days will be as the days of Lot. People went about their daily business —eating and drinking, buying and selling, farming and building — until the morning Lot left Sodom. Then fire and burning sulfur rained down from heaven and destroyed them all. Yes, it will be business as usual, right up until the Son of Man is revealed." (Luke 17:28-30)

Although numerous actions can be considered evil, there exists a particular example of evil that characterized Lot's Day.

God was aware of the condition of that depraved social system and culture.

When God judged and destroyed Sodom, the sexual immorality that was prevalent during that era was the main evil mentioned in the Bible.

As stated in Genesis 19, the sexual immorality in question was homosexuality.

Jude the Apostle reveals what God considers wickedness to the point that He must intervene in the affairs of humanity when it has reached its maximum level of debauchery. (Jude 1:14-19)

Again, the Apostle Jude gives an illustration of the wickedness that causes God's wrath to fall:

Sodom and Gomorrah and the surrounding towns had filled every sexual perversion and immorality, serving as a warning of God's eternal judgment. These cities were destroyed by fire." Jude1

A warning to the generation in which we live, which will see the end come.

What is the book of Revelation

The Revelation of Jesus Christ

A detailed list of events was revealed to God's people.

An inventory of things that "WILL" transpire.

An order of events that "Will" happen soon (on God's schedule).

An angel showed John a register of events that would come to pass on earth in the last days.

God's Word is the Book of Revelation.

It is the testimony of God's Son, Jesus Christ.

As Jesus was talking to His disciples, a question was asked, "What will be the sign of your coming and the end of the age?'

His reply, as found in Matthew 24:32-33.

There will be a generation during the last days that will witness the signs of the end times beginning to take place.

Revelation 13: Give Six Major Signs That "Will" Come to Pass:

A Worldwide Power will be Established; Ten kings will give their Power to the Beast.

"Power was given to the Beast over all kindreds, tongues, and nations." Revelation 13:7.

An individual will rise to power and will be given Authority Worldwide—the Antichrist.

A Worldwide False Religion Will be Established—Revelation 17.

All unbelievers left on Earth will worship the Beast.

From what has already transpired of the unbiblical worldwide ethic, it appears that the Woke culture, LGBTQ, Abortion, etc., are some of the characteristics of what is spoken about in forming a One-World Religion called "Mystery Babylon."

There Will be a Global Population Reduction

AI, a computerized statue that speaks (image of the beast), will order the death of all those who do not bow down and worship the talking statue of the Beast. Revelation 13:15

There Will be a Worldwide Marking System

It will be a mandatory "mark" (ID) that identifies all those who support the worldwide government.

Revelation 13:16

There Will be a Worldwide Economic System

Everyone on Earth will be required to take the mark under the Global system to buy or sell, to survive in society. Revelation 13:17

The primary aim of digital currency is to replace cash.

It is fair to say that we are indeed that generation spoken of, seeing the formation of those "signs" spoken of coming to pass.

"And when you see all these things come to pass, look up and lift your heads, your redemption draws nigh!" Luke 21:28

13

The Last Chapter Unfolds

As Revelation's Blueprint pages unfold and the coming storm spoken of in ancient prophecy looms ever nearer – not as a metaphor, but as a divine reality; Seals break and trumpets blast across the heavens, signaling judgment that no power on Earth can withstand.

The nations are drunk on Babylon's deception and gather under one global power, trading sovereignty for rebellion as corrupted governments and humanity bow to the Antichrist's dominion.

The rising "Great Reset" under the rule of the Revelation 13 Beast system will not stand but fall with great violence as foretold.

However, amid the shaking of all that can be shaken, a remnant remains secure, sealed by the Holy Spirit and anchored in truth.

Their hope is not in earthly escape but in divine rescue.

Before the foretold wrath of God rains down from heaven in full measure on an unbelieving and rebellious world of wicked humanity, the Lord will faithfully gather His own, catching them away into the portals of heaven in the "Blessed Hope," the Rapture, sparing them from the hour appointed for Judgment during the Seven Year Tribulation, also known as the Time of Jacob's Trouble, and Daniel's Seventh Week.

Once again, "When they say Peace & Safety, then sudden destruction falls upon them." 1Thessalonians5:3

All UN member states met on July 27-28, 2025, to discuss peace and safety in the Middle East. A two-state solution is what they all agree on. They will resume their meeting in September to finalize their vote.

Of course, President Trump and the Prime Minister of Israel disagree and will never agree to dividing the land in Israel.

On July 28, a powerful earthquake, measuring 8.8, occurred off the coast of Russia. Is God sending a strong message to the nations of the world, His disapproval of dividing His land, Israel, by allowing such a powerful earthquake on July 28th, the last day of their meeting?

I believe the timing of that earthquake is an indicator of what is to come upon a rebellious world, ignoring all the warnings set by the Highest.

With the weakening of America by the soon coming Antichrist supporters, and the Rapture occurring, Israel will then agree to the Peace covenant that the Antichrist then oversees that the UN has drawn up, and the most devastating time in history, the world will endure, the Tribulation begins.

God is against the dividing of His land, which He gave to Israel. Apostle Paul's writings are sure of that.

Jesus Christ is our only hope. He is God's only Son and serves as a bridge between the Father and all humanity.

He has paid the price for our redemption by taking all the sins of the world upon Himself and shedding His blood on the cross for us so that we can have eternal life with Him. If you have not received Jesus as your Lord and Savior, do so before the Judgments fall, and it's too late!

14

Reflective Questions

What truths in this book stirred your heart most deeply?

Where have you seen shadows of the prophecies in your life and community?

What actions compel you to take, considering this revelation?

What patterns in current trends mirror the vision of the Book of Revelation?

Does this book challenge your perspective on the spiritual warfare unfolding in our world?

In what way is Revelation's Blueprint & the Storm Coming already visible in modern events?

15

Notes

Chapter 1 – Watchmen and Those Watching- Understanding the Call of Ezekiel- by Francis –"Watchman on the Wall: Understanding the Call of Ezekiel 33:7" – Study Bible

"Discerning the Signs of the Times _Mike Bennett- https://lifehopeandtruth.com/prophecy/end-times/discerning-signs-of-the-times/

Chapter 2 – Peace and Safety – "How Trump's Peace and Strength Policy is Securing Peace Around the World"- The American Spectator- https://spectator.org/how-trumps-peace-through-strength-policy-is-securing-peace-around-the-world/

"Trump announces another Peace Deal, this one in the Democratic Republic of Congo" – USA Today- https://www.usatoday.com/story/news/world/2025/06/27/trump-basks-in-another-peace-deal-this-one-in-africa/84383556007/

"Could Trump's Push for Peace Be the Peace and Safety before the End"- Last Days Living-https://lastdaysliving.com/2025/02/20/could-trumps-push-for-peace-be-the-peace-and-safety-before-the-end/

"Netanyahu, Trump meet in White House, Hopeful of Peace in Gaza-UPI News-Netanyahu, Trump meet in White House, hopeful of peace in Gaza.

"Sanhedrin Mints Silver Half Shekel with Image of Trump and Cyrus" -Israel 365 News- https://israel365news.com/321845/sanhedrin-temple-movement-issue-silver-half-shekel-images-trump-cyrus/#google_vignette

"Sanhedrin sends Strong Support Letter to President Trump"-Israel 365 News- Sanhedrin Sends Strong Support Letter to President Trump – Israel365 News.

Chapter 3- 2027 Earth Changing Events- "Will Apophis Hit Earth in 2029? Will Know in 2027, Scientist says." – Forbes-Will 'Apophis' Hit Earth In 2029? We'll Know In 2027, Scientist Says

"Tucker Carlson Stunned as ex-Bush official reveals US has doomsday bunkers for elites" – Daily Mail- Tucker Carlson stunned as ex-Bush official reveals US has doomsday bunkers for elites | Daily Mail Online

"Catherine Fitts: The Oncoming Extinction Event" – Tucker Carlson Podcast-https://www.bing.com/videos/riverview/relatedvideo?q=Tucker+Calson+interview+Catherine+Austin+Fitts+says+170+cities+underground&mid=1E507EFCA1ADCD3219861E50

Chapter 4 – Wars and Rumors of Wars & Chaos-"Matthew 24- bible hub- Temple Destruction and other Signs" Matthew 24

"Hamas History"-Global Security.org- HAMAS History

Iranian "sleeper cells": What to know about US warnings-The Hill- Iranian 'sleeper cells': What to know about US warnings

"Noticing the Muslim slaughter of Christians is 'Islamophobic, ' Says the United Nations – Noticing the Muslim Slaughter of Christians Is 'Islamophobic' Says the United Nations – The Stream.

"Marxist Tantrums are nothing New" – Texas Public Policy Foundation- Marxist Tantrums Are Nothing New – Texas Public Policy Foundation.

Chapter 5- Business as Usual- Luke 17:30 Bible hub-Luke 17:30 It will be just like that on the day the Son of Man is revealed.

"America unrecognizable and on the brink of collapse, experts warn: Turning on our own Legacy' America 'unrecognizable' and on the brink of collapse, experts warn: 'Turning on our legacy' | Fox News

"The Covid-19 Pandemic- 5Years Later"- Young Americans Against Socialism-

- The Pandemic, 5 Years Later — Young Americans Against Socialism

"House panel concludes, Covid-19 came from Lab Leak"-Science- House panel concludes that COVID-19 pandemic came from a lab leak | Science | AAAS

Ending Radical Indoctrination for K-12 Schooling – The White House- Ending Radical Indoctrination in K-12 Schooling – The White House

Gender Indoctrination for 4th and 5th Grades at Oakridge
– Gender ID Indoctrination for 4th & 5th Graders at Oakridge

"Indoctrinating Children into the Demonic"- Tom's Substack- Indoctrinating Children Into The Demonic: Total Rethink Of 'Education' Is Needed

"Gender Identity Policy under Biden" The Federalist- Gender Identity Policy Under the Biden Administration

"Protecting Children from Chemical and Surgical Abuse"- The White House- Protecting Children from Chemical and Surgical Mutilation – The White House

Chapter 6 -Doers of Evil and the Beast System-

Thousands of Russia Hoax Documents Found in FBI Secret Room in Burn Bags. – The Federalist- Thousands Of Russia Hoax Docs Found In Hidden FBI Burn Bags

"The White House Press Release-At USAID, Waste and Abuse Runs Deep" The American Presidency Project-White House Press Release-At USAID, Waste and Abuse Runs Deep | The American Presidency Project

'US Agency Funds Overseas Sex Changes'- American Faith- U.S. Agency Funds Overseas Sex Changes – American Faith

"One Big Beautiful Bill Act: Tax Deductions for Working Americans and Seniors"- IRS- One Big Beautiful Bill Act: Tax deductions for working Americans and seniors | Internal Revenue Service

US Taxpayer gave Hamas millions: "Like US subsidizing Nazi Germany with the Marshal Plan before Hitler fell during World War 11"- Ynet Global- https://www.ynet-news.com/article/s1yecbioke Hitler fell during World War 11

"Politico, AP, and NY Times received millions in USAID funds? New MAGA Allegations"- Times Now World- https://www.timesnownews.com/world/us/us-news/ politico-associated-press-new-york-times-received-millions-in-usaid-funds-new-usaspending-allegation-article-117958909

"Reschenthaler uncovers $1.1 Million Taxpayer Funding Sent to the Wuhan Institute of Virology"- Guy Reschenthaler- https://reschenthaler.house.gov/media/press-releases/ reschenthaler-uncovers-11-million-taxpayer-funding-sent-wuhan-institute.

"At USAID, Waste and Abuse Runs Deep"- The White House- At USAID, Waste and Abuse Runs Deep – The White House

"The World Economic Forum 2025: Key Themes at Davos"- UBS-World Economic Forum 2025 | Collaboration for the Intelligent Age | UBS Nobel Perspectives

"Why Regulating AI can be straightforward, when teamed with eternal vigilance"- WEF- Regulating AI can be straightforward, with eternal vigilance | World Economic Forum

"Transhumanism Klaus Schwab and Dr. Yuval Noah Harari Explain the Great Reset and Transhumanism's agenda"- Zeee Media-Transhumanism | Klaus Schwab and Dr. Yuval Noah Harari Explain The Great Reset / Transhumanism Agenda – Zeee Media

"Spyware and AI: a Dangerous Evolution"-LinkedIn in-https://www.linkedin.com/pulse/spyware-ai-dangerous-evolution-eckhart-mehler-qklef

"How the pro-criminal policies embraced by the Biden/Harris administration have endangered Americans"-The Committee- How the Pro-Criminal Policies Embraced by the Biden-Harris Administration Have Endangered Americans: Report | House Judiciary Committee Republicans

"2023: The ABCs of CBDC, the Great Reset and More Centralized Control" -Gold Eagle- 2023: The ABCs of CBDC, the Great Reset(s) & MORE Centralized Control | Gold Eagle

"World Leaders Agree to Implement Vaccine Passports"-Liberty Council-World Leaders Agree To Implement Vaccine Passports – Liberty Counsel

"Mexico makes biometric identifier mandatory for all citizens" – Biometric Update- https://www.biometricupdate.com/202507/Mexico-makes-biometric-identifier-mandatory-for-all-citizens?fbclid=IwY2xjawLrk

"Transforming our World: for the 2030 Agenda of Sustainable Development" – United Nations- Transforming our world: the 2030 Agenda for Sustainable Development | Department of Economic and Social Affairs

"America unrecognizable and on the brink of Collapse, experts warn: Turning on our legacy."-Fox News, 2023-America 'unrecognizable' and on the brink of collapse, experts warn: 'Turning on our legacy' | Fox News

"The Intelligent Age: A time for Cooperation"- The WEF- The Intelligent Age: A time for cooperation | World Economic Forum

Chapter 7- Displayed Derision & Judicial Coup-Biden appointed Judge Blocks Trump from ending Free Lawyers for Illegals. -LIFE Zette news- https://www.lifezette.com/2025/05/judicial-coup-biden-appointed-judge-blocks-trump-from-ending-free-lawyers-for-illegals/

Who the Hell is Running the Country?- The American thinker: Who the Hell is Running the Country? – American Thinker

Autopen Scandal Deepens as New Evidence Emerges from the Oversight Project-Lifezette- Autopen Scandal Deepens as New Evidence Emerges From The Oversight Project [WATCH]

Chapter 8 – Deception End Time Signs-"Marxist Tantrums are nothing New"-Texas Public Policy Foundation- Marxist Tantrums Are Nothing New – Texas Public Policy Foundation

Democrats have repeatedly used violent rhetoric against former President: time to put President Trump in the bullseye"-Politics- https://www.foxnews.com/politics/democrats-have-repeatedly-used-violent-rhetoric-against-former-president-time-put-trump-bulls-eye?msockid=1c84a9e173d46ddf0cbdbfed72406c61

Video shows a suitcase filled with ballots being pulled after supervisors told all workers to leave. YouTube- Video shows suitcases filled with ballots pulled after supervisors told poll workers to leave.

Outrage erupts after windows are covered in Detroit during the Ballot count. – Daily Wire- Outrage Erupts After Windows Covered Up In Detroit During Ballot Count. Officials Release Statement On Alleged Reason Behind Decision.

Chapter 9-The Framework is Set-"We need Crimes Against Humanity Treaty now"- Crimes Against Humanity Treaty Now.

"Delegates grapple with the Definition of Crimes Against Humanity that Supports Future Development, Has Legal Certainty, as Sixth Committee Continues Resumed Session"-UN- Delegates Grapple with Definition of Crimes against Humanity That Supports Future Development, Has Legal Certainty, as Sixth Committee Continues Resumed Session | Meetings Coverage and Press Releases

Chapter 10- What's on the Horizon-

"NYC Zohran Mamdani Believes Queer Liberation Means Defund the Police"- 365 Bserver-Nolte: NYC's Zohran Mamdani Believes 'Queer Liberation Means Defund the Police' – 365 Observer

"Alice Bailey and the United Nations"- Way of Life Literature- Alice Bailey and the United Nations

"San Diego Bishop Celebrates LGBT all are Welcome' Mass, allows Drag Queen Activist to speak"-Life Site News- San Diego bishop celebrates LGBT 'All are Welcome' Mass, allows 'drag queen' activist to speak – Life Site.

"Canadian police warn traditional values may be a sign a person is becoming an extremist"-News- The Patriot Light

– Canadian police official warns 'traditional values' may be a sign a person is becoming 'extremist'

"After the Iran war, the quiet isn't Peace, it's a Prophetic Countdown"-The Stream- After the Iran War, This Quiet Isn't Peace. It's a Prophetic Countdown. – The Stream

About the Author

Lori Buelow is a spiritually dedicated researcher and author with over four decades of passionate study in Bible prophecy. Her work bridges ancient Scripture with today's global trends. Known for crafting messages with theological depth that stir discernment, courage, and urgency in readers navigating today's turbulent world. With a passion for truth and a calling to awaken hearts, her voice echoes a strong commitment to scripture and a yearning to guide others through life's turbulent storms with wisdom and boldness.

For more information and updates, visit her website, "Prophecy News and More.org"